4/10

TODO ACERCA DEL OTOÑO/ALL ABOUT FALL

Los animales en otoño/
Animals in Fall

por/by Martha E. H. Rustad

Traducción/Translation: Dr. Martín Luis Guzmán Ferrer
Editor consultor/Consulting Editor: Dra. Gail Saunders-Smith

Capstone
press®

Mankato, Minnesota

Pebble Plus is published by Capstone Press,
151 Good Counsel Drive, P.O. Box 669, Mankato, Minnesota 56002.
www.capstonepress.com

1 2 3 4 5 6 14 13 12 11 10 09

Library of Congress Cataloging-in-Publication Data
Rustad, Martha E. H. (Martha Elizabeth Hillman), 1975–
    [Animals in fall. Spanish & English]
    Los animales en otoño = Animals in fall / por/by Martha E. H. Rustad.
    p. cm. — (Todo acerca del otoño = All about fall)
    Includes index.
    Summary: "Simple text and photographs present animals in fall — in both English and Spanish" —
Provided by publisher.
    ISBN-13: 978-1-4296-3258-4 (hardcover)
    ISBN-10: 1-4296-3258-5 (hardcover)
    1. Animal behavior — Juvenile literature. 2. Autumn — Juvenile literature. I. Title. II. Title: Animals in fall.
III. Series.
QL751.5.R8718 2009
578.4'3 — dc22   2008034513

Editorial Credits
Sarah L. Schuette, editor; Katy Kudela, bilingual editor; Adalín Torres-Zayas, Spanish copy editor;
    Veronica Bianchini, designer; Charlene Deyle, photo researcher

Photo Credits
Bruce Coleman Inc./Warren Photographic, 13
Corbis/Buddy Mays, 21; Charles Mauzy, 19; Kennan Ward, 11; Kevin Schafer, 15; Tim Davis, 7
Shutterstock/Dainis Derics, 17; Eric Gevaert, 5; Gilles DeCruyenaere, cover; Mark C. Biesinger, 1
SuperStock, Inc./age fotostock, 9

Note to Parents and Teachers

The Todo acerca del otoño/All about Fall set supports national science standards related
to changes during the seasons. This book describes and illustrates animals in fall in both
English and Spanish. The images support early readers in understanding the text. The
repetition of words and phrases helps early readers learn new words. This book also
introduces early readers to subject-specific vocabulary words, which are defined in the
Glossary section. Early readers may need assistance to read some words and to use the
Table of Contents, Glossary, Internet Sites, and Index sections of the book.

Table of Contents

Tabla de contenidos

Fall Is Here

It's fall. Animals start
to get ready for
cooler weather.

Llegó el otoño

Es otoño. Los animales
empiezan a prepararse
para un tiempo más frío.

4

5

What Animals Do

Geese know winter
is coming. They fly
south together.

Cómo se portan
los animales

Los gansos saben que
va a llegar el invierno.
Vuelan juntos al sur.

6

7

Monarch butterflies fly south too. They find warm places to stay.

Las mariposas monarca también vuelan al sur. Buscan lugares más cálidos para quedarse.

8

Snowshoe hares change color.
Their fur starts to turn from
brown to white.

Las liebres llamadas raqueta
de nieve cambian de color.
Su pelo empieza a cambiar
de marrón a blanco.

Deer grow thicker coats.
Thick fur keeps them
warm in the cold.

A los venados les crece
el pelo más grueso. El pelo
grueso los mantiene calientes
cuando hace frío.

12

Getting Ready

Squirrels get ready
for winter too. They
hide nuts to eat later.

Los preparativos

Las ardillas también se
preparan para el invierno.
Esconden nueces para
comérselas después.

14

Honey bees make extra
honey. They store it
in their hives.

Las abejas mieleras hacen
una mayor cantidad de
miel. La almacenan en
sus colmenas.

16

Bears eat extra food.
They look for dens
to rest.

Los osos comen mucho
más. Buscan madrigueras
donde descansar.

A New Season

The animals are ready for winter. The new season will begin soon.

Una nueva estación

Los animales están preparados para el invierno. La nueva estación pronto empezará.

20

Glossary

den — the home of a wild animal; bears rest in dens in caves or hollow tree trunks.

hare — a mammal like a large rabbit with long, strong back legs

hive — a place where a group of bees live together; bees build honeycombs in hives.

honey — a sweet, sticky, yellow substance made by bees

season — one of the four parts of the year; the seasons are spring, summer, fall, and winter.

weather — the conditions outside at a certain time and place

22

Glosario

la colmena — lugar donde las abejas viven juntas; las abejas construyen panales en las colmenas.

la estación — una de las cuatro partes del año; las estaciones son primavera, verano, otoño e invierno.

la liebre — mamífero que parece conejo grande con las patas traseras largas y fuertes

la madriguera — hogar de un animal salvaje; los osos descansan en madrigueras en cuevas o troncos huecos de árboles.

la miel — sustancia dulce, pegajosa y de color amarillo que hacen las abejas

el tiempo — las condiciones a la intemperie a cierta hora y lugar

Internet Sites

FactHound offers a safe, fun way to find educator-approved Internet sites related to this book.

Here's what you do:

1. Visit *www.facthound.com*
2. Choose your grade level.
3. Begin your search.

This book's ID number is 9781429632584.

FactHound will fetch the best sites for you!

Index

Sitios de Internet

FactHound te brinda una forma segura y divertida de encontrar sitios de Internet relacionados con este libro y aprobados por docentes.

Lo haces así:

1. Visita *www.facthound.com*
2. Selecciona tu grado escolar.
3. Comienza tu búsqueda.

El número de identificación de este libro es 9781429632584.

¡FactHound buscará los mejores sitios para ti!

Índice